D0201311

# REBOUNDING FROM DEATH'S DOOR

### By

## Jeff Elliott

authorHOUSE

*1663 LIBERTY DRIVE, SUITE 200*
*BLOOMINGTON, INDIANA 47403*
*(800) 839-8640*
*www.authorhouse.com*

*© 2004 Jeff Elliott.*
*All Rights Reserved.*

*No part of this book may be reproduced, stored in a retrieval system, or transmitted by any means without the written permission of the author.*

*First published by AuthorHouse 08/05/04*
*Edited by Joni Jecklin*

*ISBN: 1-4184-6413-9 (sc)*

*Printed in the United States of America*
*Bloomington, Indiana*

*This book is printed on acid-free paper.*

# TABLE OF CONTENTS

# ACKNOWLEDGMENTS

Special thanks goes to Joni Jecklin who provided countless hours of editing and writing assistance. Her knowledge and expertise were greatly appreciated. Words cannot express my gratitude to the numerous medical personnel who assisted in one way or another saving both of my children's lives. In doing what you were trained to do, each of you changed the course of my family's lives forever. Thank you!

Finally, all my love and affection to my wife Ruth who encouraged and supported me during the many months while writing this story.

Back Cover Photos: by Lori Ann Cook, Courtesy of The Pantagraph; and Ray Mendez.

# REBOUNDING FROM DEATH'S DOOR

## BY JEFF ELLIOTT

## Prologue

The November evening was cool and crisp. The changing season signaled the beginning of a childhood dream coming true after years of heartache, sweat, and pain. As the game began, Eric found himself open for a three point shot and took it. Swish! He had made his first collegiate basket! Moments later, Eric again found himself wide open for a three point shot. This time, he was four feet beyond the three point line. Still filled with confidence from his first basket, he took the shot. Swish!! Two in a row!

At that moment, as his mother, Ruth, and I stood applauding, we were both filled with an overwhelming sense of pride.   I couldn't help but recount in my mind the mountain

of obstacles that Eric had overcome to arrive at this day.

# CHAPTER ONE - THE EARLY YEARS

Growing up, sports meant everything to me. You name it - basketball, baseball, football, tennis, track, golf; most of what I did revolved around one sport or another. As I grew older, my love of sports didn't change much. I met my wife, Ruth, fell in love, and was married in 1981. I was blessed because Ruth enjoyed playing tennis and golf as much as I did. In 1983 and 1985, respectively, our children, Jennifer and Eric, were born. As a family, we led a very active lifestyle either playing or cheering for one another. In most cases, the kids were right there by our sides. When Ruth and I played tennis, the playpen went with us, and the kids watched from the side of the court.

As Jennifer and Eric grew older, each developed an aptitude for different sports. Jennifer excelled in track and gymnastics. As an eleven year old, Jennifer placed 11th in the nation at the Amateur Athletics Union (AAU) High Jump. When Jennifer ran, people would say she ran with the grace of a deer. When she jumped, she would use her arms to propel her body upward in such a manor that she reminded you of a ballerina taking off for a pirouette. Jennifer's athletic talents were in running and jumping. In high school she continued to pursue track and went on to become the conference champion in high jump, setting seven meet records and four school records. She was a part of the 800 medley relay team which won the state championship and broke a seventeen year old state record.

As Eric grew older, it seemed clear that he was a natural athlete. By the time he was eleven or twelve, he excelled in baseball, football, basketball, swimming, and tennis. There were not yet any signs of the trials that were to come.

The summer before Eric was to enter 7th grade, he played on a traveling competitive baseball team, the Tigers, coached by a good friend of ours, Tom Jecklin. Tom was a soft-spoken coach who always seemed to bring out the best in Eric. During the summer season of 1997, one particular game carried more importance than most. The Tigers were playing the Oly Fire, a team coached by Ron Smith. With the recent purchase of our ten acre farm, the Oly Fire was a team comprised of Eric's future school teammates. Coach Smith, from the Olympia school district, was known for his team's many appearances at the state playoffs. With tryouts only one month away and a future coach to impress, Eric was determined to perform at his best. The day was perfect. The sun was shining, and the temperature was very comfortable. Coach Jecklin demonstrated his confidence in Eric by having him pitch. The day ended as perfect as it started, with Eric

3

striking out thirteen batters in seven innings. With a sense of relief and growing confidence, Eric headed to his first school tryout.

At the conclusion of 7th grade baseball tryouts, Eric found himself on the Olympia Junior High School team. He was thrilled, and we were excited for him. His preparation for school sports had begun at a very young age, and he was ready. As the season progressed, Eric was not having the success we had anticipated and had experienced while playing the same level of ball during the summer. We contemplated the reasons and felt it could be any of a number of things. Perhaps he felt intimidated by all new teammates, including a host of talented 8th graders. Or, possibly it was the adjustment to a new coach or a new school. Whatever the reason, we encouraged Eric to keep trying. Before the season's end, Eric complained of his vision looking blurry. Sure enough, a trip to the eye doctor, Dr. Andy Backus, confirmed that for the first time Eric needed a correction and would wear glasses. Looking back, we see the initial signs of impending trouble. At the time, however,

we thought we had an answer to his lack of success during fall

baseball. With his vision corrected he was ready to move on to

the next sport, basketball.

Later that fall over seventy boys tried out for the 7th

grade basketball team. After several days of tryouts, the coach

sat everyone down to read the names of the fifteen players

whom he selected to play for the team. Unfortunately, Eric's

name was not on the list. Confident that he just needed to

work harder, Eric joined a recreational league in the city of

Bloomington, just five miles from where we lived. As that

season progressed, Eric complained of headaches, dizziness,

and nausea. Though he didn't tell us at the time, we later found

out that when Eric was taken out of the game he often ran to the

bathroom to vomit, and then return to go back into the game.

Convinced that his symptoms might be caused by his vision,

we took him back to Dr. Backus. Sure enough, his vision had

worsened, and Eric needed a new prescription. As Eric finished out the season, his symptoms never improved.

Late in January of 1998, Eric's summer baseball team began indoor practice. After just a few practice sessions, the team's coach, Jan Jamison, contacted me. His words were plain and simple. "This is not the same kid I saw play six months ago." Jan noticed that Eric's swing was "off". During that season, Eric broke his finger swinging at a pitch that hit him in the hand. He had grossly misjudged the location of the ball. He also misjudged fly balls in the outfield. In addition to the changes in Eric's playing ability, Jan noticed that Eric was not his usual jovial self. Coach and player had always had a special relationship. In the past Jan teased Eric, and Eric responded with a humorous verbal comeback. But now, Eric's heart just didn't seem to be in it.

Coach Jamison witnessed what we were experiencing at home – an apparent lack of coordination that just didn't fit Eric's usual athleticism. He was still very active at home and continued to do chores, offering to help in whatever way the family needed him. However, he became what we would describe to our friends as "accident prone". Twice he broke the same glass window in the barn when he lost his balance, sending him backwards into the window. He lost ten days of playing time for his baseball team when he closed his bedroom door onto his big toe. It was common to see him stumble and fall when running. Eric had experienced a large growth spurt, and we wondered if his coordination would catch up with his height eventually.

Still concerned, we made a trip back to Dr. Backus's office which revealed that, in fact, his vision had worsened once again. Troubled about his third vision change in six months, we asked Dr. Backus if Eric's large growth spurt could produce that drastic of a decline in his vision. Eric had grown six inches in the past twelve months. Dr. Backus indicated that it was common for teenage boys who had taken large growth spurts to see a change in vision, but he suggested that we keep a very close eye on any future changes.

In the early spring of 1998, I became the pitching coach for Eric's baseball team. I had some prior experience as a pitcher. In 1986, I was invited to try out for the Giants, Brewers, and Cubs minor league organizations. Jan thought that my experience could help his pitching staff. I agreed, and within a month, outdoor practices had begun. After the first week of practice, Jan and I sat down on the bench to discuss the team's progress. Jan looked at me and said, "I still think that there is something wrong with Hoover." Hoover was a nickname affectionately given to Eric when he was younger. At two years of age, he had his forearm sucked into a Hoover vacuum cleaner, and the nickname stuck with him since.

I looked at Jan and told him, "I really think the lack of coordination is from Eric's growth spurt."

"Just the same," continued Jan, "I wish you would take him in for a check up."

At Jan's urging, I finally agreed to take Eric to our family doctor. He was suffering from chronic headaches, and we hated to see him in such pain. Under the belief that the problem was sinus related his doctor sent us home with antibiotics. The antibiotics had no affect on his frequent headaches, however. We returned to the family doctor two more times before being referred to an ear, nose, and throat specialist. The specialist examined Eric and prescribed another dose of antibiotics. Once again, Eric experienced no relief, and we phoned the doctor. We were frantic because the symptoms seemed to be escalating even with the antibiotics. Eric's headaches were now severe and were accompanied by dizziness and vomiting. Eric's doctor felt that he needed to be seen immediately. He was concerned that Eric could be suffering from a serious condition known as spinal meningitis. After ruling out meningitis, the doctor decided to give Eric a dose of steroids. Almost instantly, Eric noticed relief from his symptoms. Finally, we believed we were on the right track. Our joy was short lived, however;

Jeff Elliott

within a few days of ending the medication, Eric's symptoms
returned.

Ruth and I were becoming very frustrated. We worried
constantly, and the stress was draining. We wanted to see Eric
well again and back to his old self. Eric, on the other hand,
took it all in stride. He assumed that the pain was something
he would just have to learn to live with, similar to people who
have to deal with the symptoms which accompany allergies.
His positive attitude was amazing considering what he had been
through the past year. However, even Eric couldn't dismiss the
fatigue which was now becoming evident.

The following week we went back to the specialist, who
decided to order a CAT scan of Eric's head. A CAT scan, or
computed axial tomography, allows a doctor to use computers
in order to generate a three-dimensional image from two-
dimensional x-rays. The data retrieved provides a significantly
better view of the area scanned, providing information such as
depth, from multiple angles. Months later, we discovered that

the CAT scan ordered was for the frontal view of Eric's head. After all, treatment up to this point had focused on a connection between the headaches and a sinus-related condition. At the time, we had no idea that we were not looking at a complete scan of Eric's head. Within a few days, we reviewed the results with the doctor. As he pointed out the several cross sections of Eric's head, everything appeared to be clear with the exception of slight swelling in the sinus passages. Eric had responded to the first round of steroids, so once again, the doctor prescribed them hoping to alleviate the headaches and the swelling discovered in the CAT scan.

Just like the first round of steroids, the second gave us hope that we could soon put this nightmare behind us. Eric felt great again. In addition, his baseball team had received exciting news. They were going to play a game on Illinois State University's home field. Coach Jamison gave Eric the nod, and he pitched the game of his life. Jan looked at me on the bench and beamed, "He's back!"

# CHAPTER TWO - WHAT IS WRONG WITH MY SON?

Eric finished his medication, and life went on. I suppose that on some level we held our breaths. We had been through an awful lot to get to the bottom of Eric's illness.

Each step of the way, we had wanted to believe that we had reached the end and put his pain behind us. This time was no different. It wasn't long, though, before we got the first sign that the illness had not run its course.

During the following week at practice, I called all of the pitchers out to the mound to work on their form. When it was Eric's turn, I found his pitching to be very erratic. Jan was watching and when he could take no more, he walked out to the plate and said, "Hoovey, I am just going to stand at the plate with the bat, and I want you to concentrate on throwing nothing but strikes." Not knowing why he was so erratic, standing at the plate would provide Eric with a "strike zone" and hopefully settle him down. Eric nodded and wound up to deliver the ball. As he released it, the ball began to tail from the plate right into Jan. Jan quickly raised his arms to get out of the way, but it was too late. Thud! The ball hit Jan in the ribs and knocked him to the ground. Jan gasped, "I'm okay. I'm okay," as he stumbled to his feet. "You're not going to get out of pitching that easily, Hoover!" exclaimed Jan. "Get back up there and throw a strike down the middle of the plate." Eric nodded, smiled, and placed his foot on the rubber to deliver the pitch. As the ball flew, it looked as if it were right on target, until it reached the half way mark, at which point it began tailing into Jan again. It was as if I had just watched an instant replay.

Thud! The ball had hit Jan in the exact same spot as before. This time Jan didn't get up. Running to help Jan, I heard him gasping, "You win, Hoovey, I can't lie. That really hurt."

Pulling up Jan's shirt, I was sure that he had broken a rib or two. His entire left side of his rib cage was already black and blue. To this day, we still laugh with Jan and his wife, Kim, about how he tried to force Eric to throw strikes. If it was only a matter of willpower, I'm sure Jan's methods would have been successful, and Eric would have overcome his lack of pitching control. However, there was much more lurking in the background and months before we would understand just how devastating the consequences were yet to be.

As summer baseball came to a close, tryouts for fall baseball on Olympia's 8th grade team began. Eric made the team but found little playing time. The simple act of swinging the bat to hit a pitch oftentimes resulted in Eric stumbling and falling. He misjudged fly balls and lost his balance when pitching. In all, it was a season Eric would just as soon forget.

We sat in the stands and watched along with his teammates' parents. We searched for an answer to the question, "What had happened to our son?" This just couldn't be the same boy who grew up confident in his athletic ability. In fact, we knew it wasn't the same boy. But what had happened, and how would we help him find some measure of confidence and success in the athletics that he still enjoyed?

For the first time, we were actually relieved when the baseball season ended. Eric, though, was not one to give up. He turned his attention to basketball tryouts. This time, he was elated when the coach announced that he was among the fifteen players to make the team. None of us were surprised when Eric saw very little playing time during the first two months of the season. The same problems we had just witnessed in baseball continued to plague him - the inability to catch a ball, missing easy shots, and the constant tripping and falling to the floor.

The following month, in December of 1998, Eric woke up every morning with headaches, nausea, and/or vomiting.

Sometimes it went away after eating something, and other times it lasted all day. All of these symptoms can be associated with a sinus infection, so back to the doctor we went. Eric's sinus passages were a little swollen, so he was prescribed a dose of antibiotics. As the week passed, the antibiotics produced no change in Eric's symptoms. In fact, he became progressively worse, spending most of his time simply lying on the couch.

# CHAPTER THREE - WORST SNOW STORM IN TWO DECADES

On New Year's Eve day I had to report for my regular shift as a firefighter. My schedule is the same as all firefighters who work for the town of Normal. I work twenty-four hours on duty followed by forty-eight hours off. As I left for work I found it hard to be optimistic about the day. Eric was still sick, and the cold I had been battling for several days felt like a sinus infection. By 10:00 p.m. I knew that I was not up to my duties, and I decided that I had to go home sick. Normally the drive home was a short one, and all I could think about was getting

home and into bed.

As I walked out the door of the fire station, I was

met with an unwelcome site. My decision to go home sick

was ill-timed. We only lived about four miles southwest of

Bloomington/Normal but the road home was a little traveled

country blacktop, and as fate would have it, the worst blizzard

in twenty years had begun. As I began the drive home, roads

were starting to drift closed, and visibility was nearly zero when

I hit the edge of town. The two mile drive down the narrow,

icy blacktop road was dangerous and slow going. The road

had become one lane with occasional gusts of total white out.

On dark country roads this is especially dangerous, because

the roads are as white as the air around you. I had traveled this

route daily, and that familiarity was responsible for my safe

return home. I breathed a sigh of relief as I pulled into our

driveway. Ruth was waiting up for me and greeted me at the

front door. She was feeling stressed, because Eric was still no better. However, he was sleeping now. Both of us, exhausted

from the day, fell immediately to sleep.

Photo taken by Lori Ann Cook , courtesy of The Pantagraph


The worst blizzard in two decades hit Bloomington/Normal
on January 1st, 1999. A total of 14 inches accompanied by
high winds hit the city for three days.


The next morning I climbed out of bed to discover that

the snow was still falling. Combined with the high winds,

drifting and white out conditions prevailed. The road crews

had given up plowing the roads for now. With their experience they knew that they needed to wait until the winds and snow stopped or the roads would have drifted shut as soon as they cleared them. Twenty-four hours later, the snow fall finally ended. In all, 14 inches had fallen during the course of the three day storm, yet the winds still continued to howl.

The snow might have stopped, but the storm hadn't really ended. As I watched from the window of our house, the snow was being whipped around by the fierce winds and deposited in huge drifts. I was still at home sick, and my sinus infection had actually worsened. I now had a fever, as well. In order to return to work the next day, I knew I would need antibiotics. A trip into town would be necessary, but how was I going to get there? As I walked outside to get to the car in our detached garage, I discovered a major stumbling block. I had been worried about the condition of the roads into town, but I could see that I was not even going to make it out of our own driveway! The drifts leading to the road were three to four feet high! I had a two wheel drive Dodge pick-up truck, but even the truck would not be able to manage drifts of that magnitude.

As I surveyed the country blacktop heading north and south from our farm, I could see the first quarter mile was free from drifting snow. Our home was situated on our own ten acres of land, which was uniquely bordered by our neighbor's eighty acres of oak trees and shrubs to the east and north. With the wind blowing from the east, these acres of trees had proven to be a great barrier against drifting snow on the road. If we could shovel a path out of our driveway, then it looked like I might be able to make it to the main highway. Unfortunately, we still had those drifts in the driveway.

At the time, the only tractor we possessed was a 1949 Farmall "H", which did not have a bucket for scooping snow. This meant that we would have to shovel fifty yards of drifting snow by hand. Since I wasn't feeling well, the entire family volunteered to help me. Even Eric said he felt that he could help for a while, although we all noticed that he seemed to tire

23

much more quickly than the rest of us. About every fifteen minutes he would lie against a snow drift to catch his breath. He continued to help until we completed the job. Four hours later, we finally reached the end of the driveway.

As we were taking off our layers of winter clothing inside the house, Eric complained that he was having trouble catching his breath. It was then that Ruth noticed something terribly wrong with Eric's eyes. She called me over to look at them. Eric's eyes had become crossed, and he was complaining of seeing double. Ruth called Eric's eye doctor, who told her that sinus pressure could not cause his eyes to cross; something else was wrong. He instructed us to take Eric to the emergency room as soon as possible. Suddenly the pain and fever of my sinus infection receded as Eric's condition took precedence.

In my mind, I still didn't realize how serious Eric's condition had become. After all, we had just completed a CAT scan of what we thought was Eric's entire head, and the results were negative. However, being told to take my son to the emergency room started my adrenalin pumping, and fear of the unknown asserted itself. I knew that we had to go, but the practicalities of getting into town and back home again concerned me. I wondered to myself....when we return, how will we make it back into our driveway, which in this very short time had already started to drift closed again? So before we left, I called a local store located only a block off the main drive to the hospital and asked them if they had any snow blowers left. They had one left but were closing down the store early because no one was venturing out in the current weather conditions. Even the majority of the gas stations were closed. I convinced the owner to stay open for another half hour, so I could get there to buy the snow blower. I even gave him my credit card number over the phone and told him to have it ready at the door so I could load it and go. In hindsight, it was not necessary to spend the time worrying about getting back into the driveway at the end of the day. In fact, very little that happened that day went as I had planned.

My pick-up truck held three people, so Ruth, Eric, and I started uneasily down the blacktop road for what I hoped would be a safe trip to the hospital. As I had noticed earlier, the first quarter mile was clear. As soon as we were clear of the trees, the drifts increased to three feet, and I could see that the snow was even deeper further ahead. I had no choice, so I attempted to plow through. As we hit the first drift we slowed down tremendously, coming to a complete stop by the time we came to the second. Quickly, I threw my pick-up into reverse and backed up in the same tracks I had just made going forward. I looked at Ruth and said there was no way we could make it heading south. I continued to back up the same way we came until we had returned to our driveway. After realizing just how bad the roads were, Ruth was concerned that if we made it out, we might have to stay in town for the night. Since she didn't want to leave Jennifer alone, she was torn as to whether she should accompany us to town. I tried to reassure her that if she stayed at home with Jennifer, Eric, and I would be back later in the day. As Ruth got out of the truck, she handed me the cell phone and told me that she would wait with Jennifer, but I was to call her the minute I knew anything.

As Eric and I proceeded down the road, this time to the north, there was no drifting for the first quarter of a mile again. As we approached the beginning of the clearing, I could see the snow up ahead. I stopped back several hundred feet from the first drift. I decided to get a "running start" at the drifts. Before I took off, I glanced over at Eric, who was in obvious discomfort with his hands over his eyes. I revved up the engine and took off. As we hit the first drift, the snow flew over the top of the truck so that I was totally blinded for a few seconds. My heart was racing, but I never took my foot off of the gas. With each drift we hit, the truck's speed slowed down. When the speed was reduced to the point where I could no longer control the swerving of the tires on the snow, we finally slid off the side of the road into a drift that was over the tires and up to the wheel wells of the truck. I quickly threw the truck into reverse and then forward again hoping to find some traction, but the wheels would not move at all. After several more attempts to free the truck, I gave up and looked over at Eric. I don't even think he realized that we were stuck.

I pulled out the cell phone and called Ruth to tell her what had happened. I needed her to go start the tractor, so she could pull us out. Ruth immediately started crying. The stress and concern for Eric was wearing on us both, but I stopped her and told her that tears would not help us. She could help by warming up the tractor and simply praying for us. I hung up the phone and said to Eric, "We just need to pray now." My prayer was short, but very heartfelt. I said, "Lord Jesus, please help us."

I decided to try to see if I could budge the truck again, so I put it into drive and hit the gas. To my surprise we exploded out of that drift as if we were being pushed by a Mack truck. For the next half mile we hit drift after drift with amazing power. Each drift that we hit caused the snow to fly over the top of the truck. We were blinded again and again by the

blowing snow, but we never slowed down. I knew that what

we were experiencing was not humanly possible. I had grown

up in the Midwest and was an experienced driver in snowy

conditions. From my past career as a wildlife biologist for the

Arizona Game and Fish Department, I had spent considerable

time in the mountains. I had many opportunities to shovel my

way out of the snow in the mountains above 7,000 feet where

the snow didn't melt all winter. On one occasion I remember

being stuck thirty miles from the nearest person with the only

solution to shovel my way out. Four hours after starting, I had

shoveled a path that enabled me simply to drive back out the

way I had gone into the ditch. It seemed to me that the snow

was deeper this day, and my truck was not nearly as capable of

handling major snowfalls as the one I had in Arizona.

How was it possible that we had escaped from that

drift? As I pulled onto the main highway, I already knew that something special had just happened. I wouldn't find out just how special until later that night.

Quickly, I called Ruth to let her know that we had made it through to the main highway, and I told her that I would call again as soon as I knew anything. As we arrived in town, the only vehicles on the road were snow plows, and they were piling up what seemed to be mountains of snow. I detoured a block off the main road, where the store manager was waiting for me at the door. He had all of the paper work ready. I signed it and threw the snow blower into the back of the truck. Finally, we were off to the hospital.

# CHAPTER FOUR - THE NEWS
# EVERY PARENT FEARS

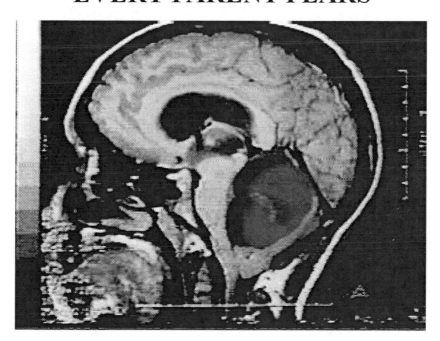

An MRI of the tumor is shown in red. Immediately left of the

tumor, notice how the Medulla is severely compressed. The

Medulla controls pulse rate, respirations, and blood pressure.

As we arrived in the emergency room, the doctors and nurses were overwhelmed with several patients who had suffered heart attacks while shoveling the snow. We waited patiently, as we understood that the most critical patients had to be cared for first. At this point, I still had no idea that Eric was actually one of the most critical patients waiting to be seen.

After about an hour, the doctor finally came into our room. As he examined Eric, he had him perform several balance tests. Eric failed even the simplest request that he touch his nose while his eyes were closed. I saw the concern on the doctor's face when he turned to me and said that we needed to go to the radiology department for an MRI. An MRI, or magnetic resonance imaging, uses radio frequency waves and a strong magnetic field rather than x-rays to provide remarkably clear and detailed pictures of tissues. The technique has proven very valuable for the diagnosis of a broad range of pathologic conditions in all parts of the body. I immediately agreed and off to radiology we went. As a firefighter, I spent much of my time on rescue runs and had come to know most of the doctors and nurses in the emergency room very well. Thus, I was allowed to accompany Eric to radiology and sit with the technician while she performed the MRI. As she conducted the test, I saw the expression on her face change to one of concern. As a parent, I'm sure that I watched closely for any indication of good or bad news, but I knew the rules. She was not a doctor, and therefore she could not tell me anything; but I knew that she had seen something and that it wasn't good.

At that moment, a man in a leather jacket and scarf poked his head around the corner and said, "I saw the light on and thought that I would see what was going on." As he came closer I still had no idea who he was, but he took one look at the screen and started giving orders to the technician. He said, "I want a reverse contrast, and I want the results hand delivered to Dr. Roth immediately. You can use my Jeep to deliver them to her." I was surprised at how he came in and totally took control of the situation. After he had finished giving his orders,

he turned to me and introduced himself as Doctor Kattner. He

told me, "The MRI has detected a very large tumor, about the

size of an orange at the base of your son's skull." He went

on to say, "We have a problem. The tumor is located in the

cerebellum (which fine tunes motor control and maintains

muscle tone), but because it is so large it is pressing up against

Eric's medulla oblongata (this controls pulse rate, respiration

and blood pressure). We need to intervene as soon as possible.

We basically have two options," continued Dr. Kattner. "We

can either operate right now, which I would prefer not to do, or

we can give Eric large doses of steroids to reduce the swelling

on his brain. This second option would give me the rest of the

day to put a surgical team together."

When I heard Dr. Kattner speak these words, it felt as if

I had a large lump in my throat, and I could not swallow. As my

eyes welled up with tears, I just couldn't believe that this was

happening to us. I could barely get the words out, but I told Dr.

Kattner that I wanted to wait until tomorrow to do the surgery, so that he could be more rested. As Dr. Kattner left the room, I was faced with two of the most difficult tasks I had ever had. First, I had to call Ruth to tell her what was happening with Eric. Then, somehow, I had to break the news to Eric.

Walking to the phone, I remember thinking that this is the kind of thing that only happens to other people. As I broke the news to Ruth, she said that she had already anticipated that something was wrong since I had not called yet. Sitting at home with nothing to do but worry, Ruth had time to mentally prepare for the news I had just delivered. It was a rare, but necessary role reversal for us. I was still sick and had been emotionally exhausted by the perils of the trip into town, so I had been blind sighted by Dr. Kattner's news. Ruth had used her time to prepare mentally and practically for the next steps she would take.

She had called our neighbors who lived up the road from us and asked who she could talk to about getting a snow plow to clear our road so she could get into town with the car. Our

neighbors knew instantly who to contact. Ruth then made the

phone call to our township road supervisor and within minutes

he showed up in our front yard with a huge Caterpillar grader

with a snowplow on the front. His father followed in a four

wheel drive pick-up truck in which both Ruth and Jennifer

could ride to the hospital. As Ruth and Jennifer followed

behind the CAT grader, they passed a state highway snowplow

which was stuck in the ditch. Road conditions were no better.

Ruth was surprised at how she had always thought the state

plow trucks were big, but this grader made them appear small.

Once in town, the CAT grader turned back to help pull out the

state plow truck, while Ruth and Jennifer continued on in the

pick-up truck.

While Jennifer and Ruth found their way to the hospital,

I was faced with telling Eric the news Dr. Kattner had given

me. By now I had composed myself and was determined to be

strong for Eric. As we sat in a private room, I said, "Eric, I am afraid I have some bad news."

Eric whispered, "It's okay, Dad. I had a mirror in my MRI machine, and I saw you crying when that man talked to you. I figured that I probably have cancer or a tumor, because I have never seen you cry before." Immediately, I was overcome with guilt knowing that Eric had to lie still for another twenty minutes in the MRI machine after watching me break down. My eyes welled up again.

"I am so sorry, Eric. I didn't know that you could see me."

There was so much to say to Eric, but now there was so little time to talk. "Eric," I said, "I know we have talked about the importance of having Jesus in your heart, but now I have to know for sure. Is Jesus in your heart? Have you accepted Him as your personal Savior?"

"He is Dad," Eric spoke softly. "You don't need to worry. I'm not afraid of dying. If I die, I'll be with Jesus;

and if I live, I'll be with you and Mom." Tears just streamed down my cheeks as I couldn't believe the courage and strength that a thirteen year old boy could possess. He was leading me through the most difficult moment of our lives, when it should have been me leading him.

Just then, Ruth and Jennifer walked in. They threw their arms around Eric and me, and we all hugged each other for a while. Then, as word spread, my Captain from the fire department, Ken Kerfoot, showed up along with our Pastor from church, Kevin Summers. Before the week ended, over 270 people stopped by to visit Eric.

As the nurses took Eric away from us into the intensive care unit (ICU), one immediate question came to our minds. Who is this Dr. Kattner and do we have the best neurosurgeon possible? It didn't take long to discover the answer to that question, as we had several very good friends on staff at the hospital. As it turns out Dr. Kattner is one of the leading neurosurgeons in the country. He studied for years under a physician in Japan who invented very specialized neurological equipment. Dr. Kattner grew up in Bloomington, IL, and just recently decided to return to his hometown to set up a specialized neurological clinic and lab. He is invited to lecture and train fellow neurosurgeons from all over the world on the use of this equipment. In fact, three days after Eric's surgery, he was in Hawaii lecturing to a group of Japanese doctors. So, did we have the best neurosurgeon for Eric? If there was to be any comfort in the fact that our son was unexpectedly scheduled for brain surgery tomorrow, it was the knowledge that Dr. Kattner was heading the team which would perform the operation. How is it that Dr. Kattner just happened to pass by Eric's MRI results? And what caused him to stop long enough and care enough, to involve himself in Eric's case? As we dealt with the emotional blow, something amazing continued to unfold. Dr. Kattner was now a part of it.

Later we received an email from Carolyn Gray, a friend of Dr. Kattner who also knew Ruth and me. She hoped to comfort us by sharing her impressions of the personal side to him. Carolyn sent an email to Ruth's sister, Julie, which read:

"I wanted to let you know that Dr. Kattner is a very special guy. His own father died of a brain tumor. It was at that time, that he decided to become a neurosurgeon. He hasn't had an easy life - but he is so dedicated - he is a Christian - he is a one in a million man! I love him to pieces. He is very special to me because I was with his dad and him when his dad died. He (Dr. Kattner) allowed me to walk down the hall with his arm around me. That was quite a privilege - even at that time. He was quite young then (I think a teenager or maybe on to college). I just love him. You may tell him that you work with me, and that I think he's wonderful."

That night, before leaving the hospital, Dr. Kattner stopped in to see Eric and us. By then Eric had experienced temporary relief from the steroids. Dr. Kattner informed us that he was successful in getting Dr. Bipin Patel, the cardiac anesthesiologist whom he had wanted to assist in the surgery.

Dr. Patel had been scheduled to do another surgery tomorrow, but Dr. Kattner convinced him to postpone it in order to assist him with Eric's operation. We did not know it at the time, but Dr Kattner was also to be assisted by Dr. Anne Stroink, another very highly respected neurosurgeon. Unbelievably we had been home just eight hours ago and now we had a team of specialists assembled with the purpose of saving our son's life.

We, of course, had not shared with Eric the extent of Dr. Kattner's concerns. He wanted Dr. Patel, specifically, because he specialized in high risk surgery. Earlier in the day, Dr. Kattner had told us that the pressure on Eric's brain was extreme. Releasing the pressure off the medulla could send him into a coma, leave him in a vegetative state, and possibly result in his death. He told me of a case very similar to Eric's in which a girl was sent home from the hospital without an MRI, and she died the same night. He believed that Eric's condition was that severe. The fact that the optic nerve had

41

been affected, causing the crossed eyes, was another devastating sign. Typically, patients with tumors this advanced die shortly after the occurrence of the symptoms. The one positive note was that the tumor was located in the cerebellum. Though the cerebellum controls balance and coordination, it is also the most "forgiving" part of the brain from which to extract the tumor. We were aware of the possible long-term effects of surgery, but we could only pray that he lived to face them.

It was now midnight, Sunday night, and Ruth and I found ourselves unable to sleep in the bunks the nurses had made for the three of us just outside of ICU. Our minds were reeling at the shock of the day, and our hearts were incredibly heavy as we worried over the fate of our son.

As Eric lay sleeping in his bed, Ruth and I decided to walk the halls and talk. We discussed many things, but eventually I began to relate the bizarre incident that occurred to Eric and me when we were stuck in the snow drift. I didn't get far into the story when Ruth stopped in her tracks and said,

"Don't say another word. Let me tell you what happened to Jennifer and me first."

"When you called to tell me to start the tractor, Jennifer and I began praying as soon as I hung up the phone. Almost instantly, I had a vision of angels descending from Heaven pushing your pick-up truck. Their bodies were transparent but shown so brightly that it made your truck a brilliant blue as well." Ruth continued, "As we were praying I wasn't even thinking about angels. I've never had a vision before, but I could see everything as if it were happening right in front of me." I was stunned and just stared at Ruth for a second or two.

Finally I could speak, and I said, "Ruth, that is exactly what happened. We were stuck in a drift so deep, that I knew it would take a tractor or some other vehicle to pull us out. But after I prayed for Jesus' help, I decided to put the truck back in drive one more time. We exploded out of that drift with such power, that I checked my review mirror to see if we were being pushed! That is it!" I exclaimed. "That explains what happened to us."

The rest of the night, neither one of us could sleep. During the remaining hours before morning, our time was spent praying, talking, and walking the halls of the hospital, making sure to check in on Eric every thirty minutes. Thankfully, the steroids were working, but their side effects did not allow Eric to sleep soundly. The next morning, surgery was to begin by 8:00 a.m. Dr. Kattner and Dr. Patel met with us around 7:00 and informed us that the surgery could take as long as eight hours even if they encountered no complications. They also warned us that when Eric awoke, he might not be able to move or talk for several hours and that it was imperative that he remain quiet and calm for several days after surgery. They reminded us that there was a chance that relieving the enormous pressure on Eric's brain could propel him into a coma. Ruth and I listened to the warnings about possible complications, but we knew that we had no choice. If Eric was to survive this tumor, the operation was essential. We continued to pray.

When the time came to take Eric to prepare him for surgery, Ruth, Jennifer, and I hugged Eric and told him that we loved him. As they rolled him away, the tears that we had fought so hard to hold back and conceal from Eric, flowed freely from all three of us. As we walked out to the waiting room, we were surprised to be met by forty family members and friends who had arrived to support us.

# CHAPTER FIVE - HE SURVIVES

Until now, I had forgotten all about my sinus infection, the reason we had begun shoveling snow twenty-four hours before. However, with no sleep during the past twenty-four hours, the effects of the infection were finally taking their toll on me. I decided to take a quick trip down to the emergency room to see a doctor and get a prescription from the hospital pharmacy. When I arrived back at the waiting room a half hour later, I was surprised to find the majority of my fellow firefighters waiting to greet me and offer words of encouragement, some even sharing their tears with me. Their support helped more than they could possibly know.

As the waiting room swelled to sixty friends and family members, it looked more like a conference than a hospital waiting room. Though we had all gathered for a single purpose, having a large gathering helped us to focus on Eric, the boy, instead of obsessing minute by minute about the status of the surgery. Even with the distractions provided by the group, it became very difficult to sit and do nothing. As firefighters, our first reactions when confronted with a crisis situation are to jump into action, take control, and solve whatever the problem might be. The waiting was in direct contrast to our training. After an hour had passed, I continued to feel the need to "do something". I announced that I was going into the prayer room and asked if anyone wanted to join me. We crowded approximately twenty people into a room that was meant to hold ten, and we all prayed our hearts out for God to save Eric.

After about three hours, one of the nurses came out of the operating room to let us know that everything was going smoothly and that they had reached the tumor through a small slit at the base of Eric's skull. Then came the task of resecting the tumor one piece at a time and pulling it back out through the slit. Throughout the course of the morning and early afternoon, many more friends stopped by to visit. Finally, after six hours, Dr. Kattner and Dr. Stroink appeared from the surgical room door drenched in sweat. They both looked exhausted but told us that everything went very well. Dr. Kattner admitted that in all of his prior surgical cases, he had never seen a person survive with that much pressure on their brain. Both Ruth and I went to embrace and to thank them, when they stepped back and said, "It wasn't us. Someone else had a hand in this." We knew that he was referring to a power beyond that which defied human explanation. Still, we told them that we couldn't thank them enough. How do you properly thank someone for saving your son's life? One year later, in an interview with the PAX

TV producers of *It's a Miracle*, Dr. Kattner said how surprised he was when he initially saw the tumor on the monitor, that Eric was still alive.

Shortly after Dr. Kattner and Dr. Stroink left the waiting room, Dr. Patel came out and appeared almost giddy. With a big smile on his face he told us that Eric was awake, speaking, and moving all of his limbs. Dr. Patel told us that he was concerned at first, as Eric was not waking up. One of the recovery nurses, Becky (a good friend of ours), asked the doctor to let her try. Dr. Patel related, "It was very odd that he opened his eyes to the name of Houb….or Herb…"

Upon hearing Dr. Patel's comment, the entire waiting room erupted, "HOOVEY!" Becky's son and Eric played baseball together, and she knew all too well the nickname that Eric would respond to best.

We asked Dr. Patel if we could see Eric, and he agreed, but stressed to us that Eric was to remain calm at all times. As we walked into the recovery room, Eric's eyes were still closed.

When we called his name, his eyes opened and he managed a slight grin. Ruth, Jennifer and I hugged him and told him that he made it. Eric nodded with his eyes, smiled again, and told us that he was sleepy. Becky was observing, and she confirmed that he would be very groggy for awhile; we weren't to worry, because this was normal.

As we were only to be allowed short intervals with Eric, we made our way back out into the waiting room to let the large gathering of people that remained with us know Eric's outcome. After we had shared the good news with everyone, our pastor stood up and said, "We need to give thanks." The forty or so who remained with us formed a giant circle, held hands, and gave thanks to the Lord for our son's life. Ruth and I thanked everyone for their support and taking time out of their busy lives to stay with us. After we had said our good-byes to everyone, Ruth, Jennifer and I returned to Eric's bedside.

Later that evening the activity level on the floor of the hospital slowed down and the lights in the hallways were dimmed. It had been nearly forty-two hours since either Ruth or I had slept, but we had no intention of leaving Eric. He remained in ICU, and we planned to stay close. The nurses had prepared cots for us in the ICU waiting room, so we both tried to get some sleep. Not even aware that I had drifted off to sleep, I felt someone grab my arm saying, "Mr. Elliott. Mr. Elliott. Eric is calling for you." I rolled off of the cot and struggled to clear my eyes and my head. I felt as if someone had drugged me. As I followed the nurse, I still had no idea where we were going. The lack of sleep had left me totally disoriented, something I had never experienced before. Walking into Eric's room, I immediately regained my senses. The reason I was here was Eric, and his eyes were open.

Eric moaned. He told me that he was hurting. I looked at the nurse for assistance, who hearing the same thing, immediately told Eric that at the instant he began to feel even the slightest pain, he was to use the Demerol pump at his bedside. She stressed again that it was critical that he keep the pain level as low as possible for several days. The doctors did not want Eric to experience any physical or emotional stress. Eric actually apologized and said, "I'm sorry, Dad. I didn't want to be a baby about my pain, so I didn't tell the nurse that I was hurting."

I reassured him by saying, "That's okay, Eric. You have nothing to be sorry for. I love you. Now try to get some rest. I'll stay with you until you're able to go back to sleep." For a few minutes I stayed by his bedside stroking his forehead, but it wasn't long before the pain medication took effect and allowed Eric to drift back to sleep. I headed back to my cot. Knowing that Eric was resting, I was immediately able to fall asleep.

Over the course of the next several days, Eric's condition gradually improved. However, he was left with one troubling side effect of the surgery. He was suffering from double vision which his doctors hoped would correct itself with time.

Many people came to visit and distract Eric, often giving him gifts such as books, magazines, and cookie bouquets. One day Eric's baseball coach from junior high stopped by the hospital to visit. As his coach left, Eric started sobbing uncontrollably. Though he meant well, with him came all of the terrible memories of that 8th grade season. Even though Eric now knew what caused his athletic decline at that time, it did not erase the painful memories of his lack of coordination – stumbling while swinging a bat or chasing fly balls.

Hearing Eric's sobs, the nurse came running into the room exclaiming, "We have to get him calmed down! We have to calm him down immediately. Dr. Kattner said any excitement could start him hemorrhaging." Nothing we did was calming Eric down.

He continued to cry saying, "What if I can never play sports again?" We tried to reassure him that the double vision he was experiencing could dissipate once the swelling caused by the surgery went down, but that provided him with little comfort.

Just then our good friend and Eric's baseball coach from 7th grade, Tom Jecklin, walked in to visit and brought with him a very special gift. It was a tape recorder with a taped message from each person in their family. Tom and his wife, Joni, knew that Eric was unable to read due to his lingering vision problems and thought that the tape recording might be a unique gift for him. Tom sat down next to Eric and immediately had a calming effect on him. Eric had wonderful memories of playing for Tom, as his soft-spoken nature always seemed to bring out the best in Eric. After Tom found out that Eric had surgery, he reminisced about how well Eric had played for him in past years. When it was his turn to record a message for Eric, he decided to put together all of Eric's past statistics on the tape. Tom only stayed for a short time, but the tape he brought with him continued to have the perfect calming effect on Eric over the next hour.

After listening to the tape's ending, Eric looked at Ruth and me, "I may never play sports again. Will I?" he asked.

"Eric," I said, "I think it is way too soon to make any kind of judgment. You just had surgery three days ago. You are so fortunate to be alive and there are so many things in life to live for even if you can't play sports. It may be that it will take a lot of time and therapy to get you back in condition to play again, but if anyone can do it, you can." For the time being, that seemed to satisfy Eric.

Photo by Lori Ann Cook courtesy of The Pantagraph

Eric wore a patch to eliminate his double vision. He would alternate the patch from one eye to the other.

By the end of the week Eric was progressing very well in every aspect of his recovery with the exception of his double vision. Dr. Kattner had referred us to a specialist for Eric's vision. After several examinations the doctor devised special lenses and a patch for Eric to wear. Eric was to put the patch on one eye for half a day and then transfer it to the other eye for the rest of the day. This allowed Eric to eliminate his double vision, since he could only use one eye at a time. The doctor believed it could take as long as three months for his vision to return to normal. If at the end of that time the double vision had not disappeared, then he recommended surgery to move the eye back to its original location. This procedure had only a very small success rate in restoring vision. While cosmetically, it would eliminate his crossed eye, as a result of the surgery the brain might simply shut down the functioning of one of the eyes, leaving Eric with a blind spot. We hoped that he would not have to go through with this procedure.

We changed our focus to helping Eric cope with this disability until his normal vision was restored. We all began to breathe a little easier. Eric had survived. We were actually turning our attention to the practicalities, such as school attendance and home care. Little did we know that Eric's double vision was not to be the worst of our worries.

Eric wanted his picture taken in his uniform after surgery,

even though he could not play. Note how the left eye is

crossed.

Seven days after Eric's surgery, Dr. Kattner felt he was well enough to go home.  The dining room had been turned into a shrine of flowers, cookie bouquets, and balloons from friends and family to welcome him home.  Eric was released with orders not to be active for the next six months.  Knowing how lucky we were just to be bringing Eric home, we could accept that news.  Eric, however, was not at all happy to hear it.  Specifically, Dr. Kattner had told him that he should do no running.  Actually, walking was okay only if he was moving at a slow pace.  He did not want Eric to elevate his blood pressure or increase his heart rate.  This he asked of the boy who was already trying to figure out how long before he would be back to his basketball team!  Over and over for the next few weeks Eric tried to convince us that he felt just fine, as if we would then ease his restrictions and he would be up and running again.  We insisted, though, that he follow his doctor's orders.  Being Eric, he followed orders but pushed himself to the limit of every restriction that he had.  He begged us to allow him to dress in uniform for his final 8th grade playoff game, even if it meant that he had to remain seated on the bench. We gave in, and his crossed eye was still evident in the individual picture taken at the game.

# CHAPTER SIX -THE WORDS EVERY PARENT FEARS - FOR A 2$^{ND}$ TIME

Eric had been home about a month when Jennifer developed an ear infection. Pretty routine compared with what we had just been through. She was put on an antibiotic which usually provided relief in as few as twenty-four hours. Over the next three days, Jennifer's infection seemed to get worse, not better. She had developed a fever which wasn't responding to the Tylenol we were giving her.

The fourth day of her illness was a duty day for me at the fire department. As usual, I awoke early, ate breakfast, and left before anyone had risen. About 11:30 a.m., I received a phone call from Ruth. She was very upset, calling me from the doctor's office. She quickly explained that Jennifer had come down from her room delirious, burning with fever. Jennifer had staggered down the stairs earlier that morning and asked Ruth for her order, as if she was a waitress at a restaurant. What Ruth said then was totally unbelievable. "Jeff, then she told me that she was seeing two of everything." Eric's vision had not yet shown any improvement, and now Jennifer had the same complaint. Ruth continued on, "I knew something was terribly wrong, so I gave her Tylenol and brought her directly to the doctor's office. When the nurse took her temperature she immediately reacted. The thermometer read 105.2 degrees!"

Ruth further explained that the nurse ran and got the doctor who quickly examined Jennifer and said, "We have to act now. I believe she has spinal meningitis. She needs a spinal tap at once!"

I was stunned by the news. I knew enough about medical conditions to know just how serious this was. And I immediately felt for Jennifer, because I knew that a spinal tap is a very painful procedure. However, Ruth told me that Jennifer was so delirious from the fever that she felt little pain as they withdrew the fluid. As we were talking on the phone the doctor came back into the exam room and told Ruth, "We don't have the test results back yet, but we have to treat her as if she has bacterial spinal meningitis. If we wait for the results and they are positive, she will not survive. We have no choice but to begin treatment."

Ruth returned to the phone to tell me what the doctor said and told me, "You have to get down here. They are going to take her across the street to the hospital."

As I hung up the phone, all of the firefighters had gathered around me. They had overheard just enough of the call to respond to the concern in my voice. I'm sure that they thought Eric was the source, because we still had a long road ahead of us in his recovery. When I explained to them what had happened and that this time it was Jennifer, we all stood there in disbelief for a moment. Only one month from Eric's brain surgery, and Jennifer had now contracted a serious illness. I told the captain that I had to go, even though my family sick time had been exhausted with Eric's hospitalization.

When I arrived at the hospital, Jennifer was slightly better. Extracting the spinal fluid for the test had temporarily relieved the pressure that was building against her spinal cord and brain. A few hours later, a physician, Dr. Knoll, came in and confirmed that Jennifer was indeed suffering from bacterial spinal meningitis. She went on to say that meningitis can be contracted in different ways but that Jennifer's illness was a result of a secondary bacterial infection. In other words, the bacteria which caused the ear infection had managed to work its way into the brain and spinal cord (a rare case, but it does happen). They planned to treat Jennifer with a powerful drug, Rocephin. The only other drug which is effective against this type of bacteria is Penicillin, and Jennifer has a known allergy to Penicillin. Due to the seriousness of the illness and its highly contagious nature, Ruth and I we were given antibiotics as a precaution along with the rest of the hospital staff that came into contact with Jennifer.

As the day went on the Rocephin seemed to be working, and Jennifer showed signs of improvement. She was sleeping most of the time, but her fever had been greatly reduced. Another crisis averted, one of us had to leave to go home and stay with Eric through the night. I decided that I should go, and Ruth could spend the night in the bed next to Jennifer.

At home, I discovered that Eric was fine. He wanted very badly to visit Jennifer in the hospital, but I explained how dangerous it was for him. "Jen's illness is highly contagious, Eric. In your weakened condition, if you were to catch this from Jennifer, it would kill you. You cannot risk anymore swelling to your brain." Eric understood, but he wasn't happy. Jennifer had stood by him, and he wanted to be there for her.

67

At midnight, I jumped out of bed to the sound of a loud ringing. It took me several seconds to realize that it was the phone. As I gathered my senses, I heard Ruth's voice on the other line. I knew it couldn't be good to be getting a call at this time of night. "Jeff, we have a problem. Jennifer has rejected the Rocephin. She is broken out all over her body in hives."

"Oh, no!" I exclaimed. I just couldn't believe that this was happening to us again.

Ruth continued on, "Dr. Knoll wants to talk to you to explain our final option." It was impossible to ignore that Ruth had used the word "final."

"Hello, Jeff," Dr. Knoll spoke softly. She continued, "I want you to know what we have to do. Since Jennifer is allergic to the Rocephin and to Penicillin, our last option is to use a combination of drugs. We need to give her Chloramphenicol, which by itself is not strong enough to fight an infection of this kind, but combined with Vancomycin, they will kill the bacteria."

68

"Okay," I said. That didn't sound too bad. But that was not all.

Dr. Knoll continued, "There is one problem with using the Chloramphenicol. Use of that drug was discontinued on a regular basis in the late 1970's because of a chance that it could produce a deadly side effect known as aplastic anemia. The chance is small. However, if Jennifer should contract this there is no cure, and it would destroy her bone marrow. She would die." I couldn't believe she would suggest this treatment option. "Absolutely not! We can't give that to Jennifer!" I exclaimed.

"You don't understand," Dr. Knoll said. "If we don't give it to her, she will die from the spinal meningitis. If we give the drug to her, at least she has a chance to live. I want you to understand that the chance is small that she will contract aplastic anemia, but there is a chance." Dr. Knoll continued, "If we begin the new drug combination this evening, we won't have to wait long to find out if Jennifer contracts the aplastic anemia. We will know by tomorrow morning through blood tests whether or not she has contracted the disease." I paused for a moment, remembering the day only a month ago when I was forced to make a similar decision. Once again, we actually had no choice.

"Okay," I said.

"All right then. I will put your wife back on," said Dr. Knoll.

As Ruth started to talk, I could tell she was crying, under her breath, so as not to disturb Jennifer. "I can't believe it!" I said.

Ruth cried, "What are the chances of having two kids with different life threatening illnesses, both of whom have double vision, let alone one month apart?" We consoled each other for the next few minutes and then decided that there was nothing more we could do until morning. We agreed that we would both try to get a few hours sleep, and I would be back first thing in the morning.

At 6:00 a.m., my alarm clock went off.  It felt as if I had just lain down to sleep.  I quickly showered, checked in on Eric to make sure he was fine, and then took off for the hospital. I arrived at Jennifer's room by 7:00 and found Ruth already awake. "The drugs are not as strong.  She is not doing as well as she was," Ruth said.  I put my hand on Jennifer's head but got no response.  I could not tell whether she even knew that I was there. Ruth looked at me and said, "Dr. Knoll is still here. She never went home last night."

"I am going to go talk to her," I whispered to Ruth.

As I walked down to the nurses' station, I could see that Dr. Knoll was surrounded by a team of doctors, one of whom I recognized to be a doctor of immunology.  "Hi, Dr. Knoll," I said quietly.  "What is going on?"

Dr. Knoll responded, "I thought you had enough to worry about last night and it was late, so I didn't want to discuss this with you then.  I have called in a team of immunologists to figure out what we should do if Jennifer's body rejects this last drug. We have been on the phone with the Center for Disease Control all night trying to work out a formula of small Penicillin doses. The desired effect would be that she would gradually build up a tolerance of the Penicillin without having an allergic reaction and yet still fight the bacteria causing the meningitis. So far it appears that the doses of Penicillin which would be safe for her to take would be too small to be effective against the meningitis." She continued, "It appears as if the current drugs we are giving her are our only answer. We are going to draw blood by 8:00 a.m. and should have the results back in a few hours. Then we will know whether or not Jennifer contracted aplastic anemia."

We prayed and were thankful that there is not a limit to the number of prayers that can be answered. For soon we discovered that Jennifer was one of the fortunate ones who had taken the drug and had not contracted aplastic anemia. We were so thankful; another immediate crisis had passed. We knew, however, that even if Jennifer responded well and recovered from the meningitis, it was likely to leave some serious problems in its wake. We simply prayed for her recovery, knowing that we would deal with the problems when they surfaced.

In all, Jennifer spent eleven days in the hospital battling meningitis. She spent approximately twenty hours a day sleeping, and twice a day her vein would collapse at the site of her intravenous (IV) injection due to the strength of the drugs. She had twenty-seven IV sticks during her stay, and when she left the hospital she looked like a pale bag of bones. But we were going home, and she was going with us. That is all that mattered.

It was great to be home. We walked inside, checked on Eric as always, and got Jennifer settled. Then, we collapsed in the living room chairs and just stared at each other for a moment. We talked about how grateful we were that both of our children were alive after battling two life threatening illnesses only a month apart. We actually felt as if we had been through two battles. The good news, though, was that we still appeared to be winning the war. Now we would assess what

needed to be done to complete their recoveries and try to find

in ourselves as much strength as they seemed to possess.

# CHAPTER SEVEN - YEARS OF THERAPY

We wondered how the kids would possibly finish the school year with their disabilities. Eric's double vision had not improved, so reading was a real struggle. In Jennifer's case, it soon became clear that the meningitis had taken its toll on her ability to think and comprehend. She could still read but could not comprehend what she had read. Even spelling simple words like "water" or "from" were extremely difficult for her. Our family physician Dr. Kim Marshall reminded us that spinal meningitis swells the brain and leaves it bruised.

The effects might be temporary but at times are permanent. Every case is unique, and we were once again waiting to see.

In the weeks to follow, the school provided tremendous assistance to both of our children. Eric's tutor brought his work to him enlarged to the point that the words were almost one-half inch in size. Jennifer's tutor read to her and gave her oral exams. What they did not get from their tutors, they got from each other. Jennifer helped Eric with his therapy, while Eric helped Jen comprehend what she was reading. One example stands out in my mind. Jennifer had to write a paper, and from the kitchen we overheard Eric patiently helping her, saying, "Jennifer, what is it you are trying to say?"

Tutors would blow up Eric's homework so that the words were

1/2 inch in size.

Jennifer replied, "You know. It is in your cup."

"Soda?" asked Eric.

"No," answered Jennifer, clearly frustrated. "You know.

It's wet....," she continued.

"Water?" Eric tried again.

"That's it!" Jennifer exclaimed.

Eric laughed and said, "It's okay, honey. It will all come

back to you." During the remaining three months of school,

each continued to help the other. Though they had always been

close, their bond grew even stronger.

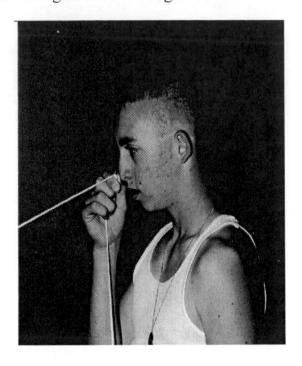

Eric performed one of his many visual therapy exercises,

using the string to make his eyes focus.


During the next several months, Jennifer's condition

continued to improve. By the start of her junior year she was

back at school and doing well. Despite her success in athletics

when younger, in her senior year Jennifer decided to focus

instead on obtaining her Certified Nursing Assistant License

(C.N.A.). Inspired by the treatment she and Eric had received during their hospital stays, Jennifer was focused on obtaining a nursing degree. She would be able to use the C.N.A. license to work in a local hospital while attending college. For Jennifer life had returned to normal.

Eric's progress was not as quick or as dramatic. The follow-up MRI performed a month after surgery showed no sign of any residual tumor. Three months after Eric's surgery, his double vision and crossed eye had still shown no sign of improvement. Due to the size of Eric's tumor and its location, there were not many doctors with experience in treating symptoms such as Eric was experiencing. The truth is that not many of these patients survived. We consulted with a doctor whose specialty is in neurological dysfunction, and he recommended surgery to cosmetically move the eye back to its center position. Ruth spent considerable time on the computer searching for information that might assist us in making this decision. We wanted so desperately to see Eric's condition resolved, but we didn't want to risk his sight. As parents we knew that the ultimate decision was ours. Not to be dismissed, though, were Eric's feelings about another surgery, and he didn't want it! He tried to make light of his vision problems, joking that the "patch makes me look more daring." After researching the procedure, we discovered that there was a very real risk that the surgery would not correct Eric's double vision. In fact, the surgery could cause his brain to compensate by shutting down the vision in one eye.

We were anxious for a resolution for Eric's vision dysfunction but prayed for another solution. Fortunately we learned of a physician in town, Dr. Witte, who practiced physical therapy as a treatment to correct many eye dysfunctions. We asked Dr. Witte if he thought physical therapy could be successful in resolving Eric's visual problems. He agreed to examine Eric but admitted that he had never treated anyone with a vision problem caused by a tumor.

During the initial exam, Dr. Witte conducted a series of diagnostic tests. Finally after about twenty minutes, Eric was asked to look into a light through glasses with colored lenses. Dr. Witte asked Eric to tell him what color the light appeared to be. Although Dr. Witte did not change a thing, for Eric the light alternated between two colors. Eric would say, "Now the color is green, no.... no, now it is red." The left lens of the glasses was red in color, while the right lens was green. Eric's brain was already compensating by shutting down the vision in the left eye which left him seeing only the green color in the right lens, and then it would switch to the right eye which showed him the color red from the left lens. After five minutes of this type of exchange, Eric blurted out, "Now it is a totally different color! Now it is yellow."

"Yes!" exclaimed Dr. Witte. "That is exactly what I have been waiting to hear." Dr. Witte went on to explain that Eric's brain was not using both eyes for normal binocular vision. It was negotiating the use of one eye at a time, and that was why the color kept changing from red to green. At the end of the twenty minute session with repeated exposure, Eric's brain was finally able to combine the functioning of both eyes which produced the yellow color. Dr. Witte informed us that "yellow" was the indication that it might not be too late to heal Eric's vision with therapy.

Dr. Witte excused Eric from the examining room and spoke privately to Ruth and me. He knew that it was imperative for Eric to have complete faith in the effectiveness of the therapy. He wanted to be certain, though, that we understood. He said, "I want to caution you that we are entering uncharted territory here. I have never had a case like Eric's. I don't have a timetable to give you, nor do I know if a 100% recovery is even possible. But if you are willing to try, I am more than willing to give it my best shot. If Eric is to see improvement, he will, along with you, need to be committed to its success. He will only get out of it what he puts into it. Many hours of therapy will need to be done at home, in addition to what he does in the office here." Dr. Witte didn't know Eric yet, but he would. There might not be any guarantee that the therapy would be successful, but we knew that if it failed it would not be a lack of effort on Eric's part.

Ruth and I left relieved and in agreement that we would rather Eric try physical therapy before any type of surgery. We discussed the two options with Dr. Kattner, who was still Eric's primary physician. He concurred with our decision to utilize physical therapy before surgery, but he also cautioned us not to expect too much. "You have to remember the size of Eric's tumor was so great that it may have created permanent damage to the cerebellum which controls his balance and coordination," Dr. Kattner warned. "Some of it may be relearned, but after a year, what we have left with his coordination is probably all we will ever see," he continued.

The next several months, Eric spent countless hours in therapy. Three days per week he had appointments at Dr. Witte's office. Every night he spent at least an hour practicing over and over again. Eric viewed this opportunity with tremendous hope that he could return to a normal life in sports. All he needed was to be given even the slightest chance that his dream of playing college basketball was still alive, and he would go after it with every ounce of determination he had.

The goal of this therapy was to improve Eric's coordination to its optimal level. By repeating the exercises over and over, beyond even what the doctor required, Eric attempted to re-teach his brain the coordination skills that had been destroyed by the tumor. As in learning any new skill, Eric needed to provide the brain with a building block of knowledge formed by repetitive experience. The therapy was also designed to strengthen the muscles of his eye in order to move his eye back into focus, not only for the cosmetic appearance of the eye, but with the ultimate goal of improving his coordination.

One of Eric's first assignments was to simply walk on a flat piece of toilet paper. Initially, Eric could not even take one step without "falling off". The realization hit us all hard. He had such a long way to go in regaining his coordination.

One night, discouraged by his short-term lack of progress, Eric came to me for encouragement. The only thing I could think to do was rent the movie, *Rudy*. After watching it as a family, I turned to Eric and said, "If your dream of playing basketball again is to come true, then you will need to have the 'heart' of Rudy."

Inspired now, Eric replied, "You're right, Dad. I can't give up. I've got to keep trying." That was all the inspiration Eric needed. He was back at his therapy with renewed enthusiasm and the vision of Rudy's success for motivation.

As Dr. Witte got to know Eric, he created exercises that reflected Eric's interests. He knew that it would be easier for Eric to keep his focus and be successful if he structured the exercises to include skills Eric used in the sports he had played.

Dr. Witte devised a drill which required Eric to shoot free throws. I'm sure Eric will never forget the first session. Using one eye, Eric's first shots were all four feet to the right of the rim. It was heartbreaking to watch, and Eric was very, very frustrated. But he would not give up! A week of shooting baskets, and he was able to make a free throw. His consistency improved, so he switched the patch over to the other eye; he began the process again. Over the course of many weeks, the adjustment period began to narrow. He could switch the working eye more frequently. He was retraining his brain and actually moving his eye slowly back into its normal position. Each small but distinct step was a victory and caused him to push himself harder and harder.

Another exercise that Eric loved involved golf. Eric had to wear his colored lenses and then putted the golf ball. As the ball rolled, Eric tried to focus on it and make the color appear yellow. In the months that followed, the exercises became increasingly more difficult. Instead of following a slow moving golf ball, he eventually had to follow a white wiffle ball pitched underhand to him, eventually catching it and later, hitting it.

During Eric's physical therapy, Dr. Witte made him special prism glasses which when worn, eliminated Eric's double vision. Each month he experienced great improvement which led to a constant reduction in prism lens strength. Still, Dr. Witte told us that when Eric's vision returned to normal it might happen suddenly and unexpectedly.

One night as our entire household slept, Ruth awoke to the sound of Eric's feet on the old creaky wood floor above our bedroom. Instantly Ruth's thoughts flashed back to the time when Eric was sick. In the back of her mind lurked the fear that the symptoms from the tumor (vomiting at night, headaches, and the inability to sleep) might someday return. She made her way as quickly as possible to Eric's bedroom and could see light being emitted from under the door. With trepidation she slowly opened the door to see what appeared to be Eric sleepwalking. He walked around the room and looked at the numbers on the alarm clock for several seconds before

moving on. He stepped over to some of his pictures and stared

for seconds at each one. Finally Eric glanced at Ruth and said,

"Mom, I just can't believe it. My vision is single! I have been

walking around the room looking at everything to make certain

that it is real and that I'm not dreaming."

"Eric, that is fantastic!" exclaimed Ruth. Eric had

trouble going back to sleep that night. He was afraid that if he

closed his eyes and went back to sleep, the double vision which

had plagued him for so long would return. It never did.

At the end of one year of therapy, Eric's vision was nearly

perfect. Dr. Witte was so excited that he asked for permission

to publish Eric's results. We were so thankful to this man and

his staff for their innovative approach to Eric's therapy. As

Doctor Witte and his assistant, Carol Kashian later wrote:

"At the time Eric was seen, he was wearing a pair

of glasses with a patch over his left eye. He told me that it

not only blocked the double vision, but made him look more

daring. This will give a clue as to Eric's amazing attitude. He was a thirteen year old male, going through all of the normal stuff associated with that age, and was now burdened with the cosmetically unacceptable need to look so radically different. With all that had happened to him, his sense of humor never left him." Visual therapy was started on the 24th of March, 1999. All of the procedures and activities that were recommended were done with a level of enthusiasm that is truly rare for one of his age. Activities that most young people would balk at because of the infantile level were done many times more than asked. Even when asked to try to walk on a strip of toilet paper and failing many times, Eric kept at it - even videotaping it to show his performance. It is a rare individual that would throw themselves into such a training program and stay with it regardless of the amount of time it required. Eric never quit or wavered in his desire to not only return to "normal", a stretch for him, but wanted to excel. He never wanted to quit until he had achieved improvement in a given skill or activity...Only through his determination and drive did Eric achieve the results

he wanted. Going from double vision by a crossed eye posture,

demonstrating no depth perception and very inaccurate spatial

organization, Eric slowly and surely achieved his goal. Last

seen, Eric demonstrated normal depth perception without the

need for prisms, and a fully functional binocular visual system…

Eric's progress was phenomenal due to his determination and

drive…It was with reluctance that we released him from our

office to return him to his regular optometrist."

# CHAPTER EIGHT - MEDIA ATTENTION

As news spread of Eric's tumor and the events that surrounded it, a reporter from the local newspaper, Paul Swiech, contacted us about doing a story on Eric's illness and his recovery. I shared with Paul the experience Eric and I had of being stuck in the snow storm and Ruth's vision of the angels pushing Eric and I free. After we had finished telling the story to Paul, he said, "I have to ask you. How do you know that this is a miracle from God?"

I told him, "Well, if it is a miracle from God, then He would make sure the story is told and if it isn't, then I am sure it will die on its own." It's not that miracles have to be made public to be valid; in fact, I believe miracles happen everyday, many of which remain untold. What I wanted Paul to understand by that was that even though we had not contacted the media ourselves to tell our story, we continued to receive requests from others to make it public. We knew that God had a hand in Eric's survival, and the fact that we were being contacted to tell the story, I felt, was a gentle nudging from God that He wanted the story told. I am not sure that Paul agreed with my explanation, but a year later, we once again had the same conversation.

Shortly after our interview with Paul, he contacted Dr. Kattner and asked him about our belief that the unusual set of circumstances that save Eric's life was a miracle. Dr. Kattner's response published on January 31, 1999 in our local newspaper "The Pantagraph" was so unique. He simply stated "Medical science doesn't know everything. Anybody who believes that is quickly made a fool of." While my respect and admiration for Dr. Kattner were already great, I could hardly believe a world renown neurosurgeon would say something so profound. It is a rare individual whose wisdom equals his intelligence.

Later that summer, we were contacted by a writer from a magazine called *Angels on Earth*. The writer told us that people with whom we attended church were inspired enough by Eric's story to submit it to their magazine. Eric seemed comfortable with the idea, so we agreed. They told us that they would be sending out photographers from the Chicago area to take our pictures.

Eric sat on the truck bed at the photo shoot for "Angels on Earth" magazine.

On the day that they were to arrive, I thought I would get some chores done with the horses. One of the reasons we had purchased the farm was to breed and raise horses as a second part-time business. My goal was to breed enough horses that I could have a horse farm when I retired from the fire department. That morning, one of my mares was in heat, so I thought I would try to breed her before the photographers arrived. Often, when mares are in heat, they become unruly. Such was the case this day with my mare called "Blaze". As soon as I opened the stall gates, Blaze burst through and was loose. "Of all days for this to happen," I thought to myself. I chased Blaze for over four hours across several hundred acres of my neighbor's fields. By 2:00, the photographers had arrived, and we were all a sweaty mess from chasing Blaze who, by the way, was still not back in the corral where she belonged. Ruth met them in the drive and asked if they could wait for a little while.

They agreed to wait saying, "This is great. We are from the city and have never seen any kind of a round up in real life." I chuckled to myself. What they thought was entertainment, was pure misery and stress for all of us.

During the next half hour, I was fortunate to get Blaze headed back in the direction of our farm. Ruth and Jennifer had the corral gates open. In my truck now, I circled around Blaze from the rear. I gently accelerated my truck at Blaze, and she responded the way I had hoped. She was heading in the direction of the farm. As the photographers watched, they asked Ruth if they could help. Ruth had them form a human fence leading right into the corral. At first Blaze balked and turned to run past me. I quickly slammed the pick-up into reverse and sped backwards to get behind her again. As my tires spun, I created my own dust cloud much to the amusement of the photographers. As soon as I sped past Blaze, she once again turned and galloped toward the human funnel leading into the corral. This time it worked. I quickly hopped out of the truck to close the gate, but Blaze was quicker. She turned to run past me. Quickly, I lunged for the lead rope that was still attached to her halter. The rope burned my hands as it slid all the way to the end where a knot enabled me to gain a firm grasp. This time I wasn't going to let go. I dug in my feet while Blaze dragged me another ten yards before coming to a complete stop. I slowly calmed her down with my voice and then led her quietly back into the corral. The excitement was finally over, and the photographers had actually been a part of a real "round-up".

Once ready, we accompanied the photographers to a local golf course called The Den. They chose this location because Eric had often used their practice green for the putting exercise which was a part of his therapy. Management at The Den agreed to let us set up off to the side of the # 1 tee box for our photo shoot. The day before had been the first tournament hosted by the course, and Arnold Palmer, the course designer, had been present. As Eric and I posed by the first tee box, Ruth and Jennifer stood back several feet where she overheard golfers getting reading to tee off and talking amongst themselves. "Yes, he does have blonde hair just like Arnold. Yes, I am sure of it. He must be Arnold's grandson."

Later that night, the photographers, Ruth, Jennifer, Eric, and I all went out for dinner at a local restaurant, where Ruth shared the story with us. The presence of the photographers had given those golfers reason to believe that Eric was famous, especially considering the event which had occurred the day before. As we dined, the reflection of the days' events, though stressful at the time, now gave us a reason to share laughter with each other.

# CHAPTER NINE - A SMALL PIECE REMAINS

In December of 1999, Eric's first "routine" MRI was scheduled. Dr. Kattner had recommended an MRI every six months to make sure that there was no evidence that a piece of the tumor remained. If there was no evidence that the tumor remained or showed signs of re-growth within five years, then chances were excellent that Eric would not have a recurrence. He was doing great, and I remember feeling confident that everything would be fine. I was wrong.

Within an hour of the appointment, Ruth called me to let me know that the MRI showed evidence that a small residual piece of the tumor remained in Eric's brain. As Ruth told me the news, I felt my heart sink once again. "How is it possible that there is still a piece of the tumor there?" I asked. Dr. Kattner later explained that depending on the location, some surgeries will result in a small residual piece of the tumor that could not be seen at the time of the surgery, or re-growth could have taken place.

The news devastated Ruth and me for weeks to come. We understood that surgery might be necessary once again. Due to the location of the small piece of the tumor, it would be difficult to remove it through traditional means, but Dr. Kattner remained confident that if it was necessary he would find a way. The other alternative was to remove it through radiation therapy. However, radiation had some serious drawbacks due to the tumor's location. It was very difficult to know that a piece of something so destructive remained in Eric, but for now we decided not to have any further surgery. Dr. Kattner would monitor the tumor for any future growth with a semi-annual MRI. If no growth occurred, we would proceed as normal.

Photo taken by Steve Smedley, courtesy of The Pantagraph

Jeff Elliott, far right, watches as the crew of It's A Miracle films a scene.

Eric took everything in stride. He remained convinced that one day he would return to play basketball, with the ultimate goal to play at college. During the next school year,

Eric entered his freshman year at Olympia High School. With this came the one question that occupied Eric's thoughts. "Can I play sports again?" We knew that football was definitely out. At the base of Eric's head was a two inch long piece of skull about the width of a piggy bank slit, which was missing. Due to the location of several blood vessels at the incision site, Dr. Kattner was unable to replace the bone or even graft a plate in its place. With this piece gone, Eric could not take the constant blows to the head that a football player endures. Eric had already accepted this, but his question was, "Can I play golf, basketball, and baseball?" Eric was thrilled and so were we when Dr. Kattner gave Eric the green light to play the three sports that he desired. Dr. Kattner later wrote the following about Eric:

"The tumor that Eric had is known as a pilocytic astrocytoma. These are typically benign tumors histologically but can be malignant clinically. In Eric's case if this tumor was not treated it would have resulted in his eventual death.

Eric's tumor was extremely large for this type of lesion. It was certainly much larger than most pilocytic astrocytomas that are diagnosed. In addition, the location of the tumor obstructed the flow of spinal fluid resulting in a condition known as hydrocephalus. The combination of the large tumor and the hydrocephalus resulted in severe brainstem compression. In many cases this results in sudden death. It is not surprising that Eric had residual effects after surgery such as diplopia (double vision), perceptual problems, balance and coordination even one year after surgery. Tumors near the brainstem frequently result in these symptoms. In most circumstances, these deficits are permanent at one year following surgery. It is rather surprising that Eric's deficits eventually went away, so that he was able to return to competitive sports. This is very unusual and is a testament to Eric's determination to lead a normal life."

As the fall season began, the first sport to test Eric's recovery was golf. As tryouts neared the end, Eric was elated.

He had made the team with a 92 average. The season was a fun one for Eric as he enjoyed just being able to compete again.

As the basketball season began, we would see a different side to Eric's recovery. Eric received very little playing time and when he did get into the game, he spent most of the time falling to the floor. As we had suspected, golf was a sport that would be relatively easy for him in terms of muscle control, but when he added running, jumping, and cutting, Eric's brain responded very differently. At times it seemed as if he spent more time on the floor than he did standing. Yet, in the midst of what would be total despair for most kids, Eric maintained a very positive attitude. He knew and so did we, just how much he had been through just to be able to put that uniform back on and go out onto the court. From our standpoint, we worried. Every time he fell to the floor we were concerned that he might suffer a blow to the back of his head that was left unprotected by his skull. For Eric's sake, we tried to focus on the fact that he was able to do the things that he enjoyed so much.

During the baseball season of Eric's freshman year, he saw very little playing time due to a strain of his pitching arm. When we took Eric into the local orthopedic doctor to examine his arm, we discussed his medical history with the doctor. The doctor recommended that we take Eric to a sports enhancement program that was next door to his office. He wasn't sure if the program could take Eric to a level beyond that which had been accomplished through the vision therapy, but we had nothing to lose.

After consulting with the head trainer at the clinic, he agreed to work with Eric on a trial basis for three months, but like all of the other doctors, he cautioned us that he had never had a case like this before and could not guarantee the results.

That summer, Eric spent three days a week doing exercises he had never seen or heard of. He would come home each night after his training session, sore and tired. After three months, the results were phenomenal. Eric had increased four inches on his vertical jump, gained ten pounds, and most importantly had all of his coordination back. As he ran up and down the basketball court, he no longer fell. More than a year after his surgery, Eric still defied the odds and showed improvement where none was to be expected.

# CHAPTER TEN - RECREATED FOR TV

In the winter of 2000, we received a call from Michael Jones, the producer of a show called *It's a Miracle*. Michael told us that he had received our story from the editors of *Angels on Earth* magazine. Of the thousands of stories they receive each year, they select only a few to re-create for television. He wanted to produce Eric's story but needed permission to show up on our doorstep for several days of filming. We had watched several episodes of *It's a Miracle* and knew that each one lasted only fifteen minutes, yet we discovered first hand just how much time went into the filming of one episode.

On the first day of filming, BroMenn Hospital graciously agreed to let the production crew film right at the hospital. The hospital even allowed the camera crews to film the actual MRI scan of Eric's tumor. In all, fourteen hours of filming took place that day. Two days before they had arrived, the Bloomington area had received two inches of snow fall. That pleased the producers greatly, since most of the second day would be filmed outside in the snow.

As we left the hospital after the first full day of filming, we realized too late that all of the snow which had covered the ground when we entered had now melted. This left our producers with somewhat of a problem. They definitely needed snow for the scene where Eric and I were stuck in the pick-up truck. Our daughter, Jennifer, came up with the solution to the problem. Earlier in the week, we had witnessed semi-trucks hauling load after load of snow away from State Farm's Corporate Headquarters' parking lot. "Surely, those piles of snow haven't melted yet," suggested Jennifer.

By the next morning, State Farm had donated three semi-truck loads of snow for the film crew to use as they wanted. Also, Sturm's Snow Makers from Wisconsin, a special effects' crew, had arrived on the scene to cover the area with a type of white foam that looked exactly like snow. It was the same crew that created the special effects for the movies, "The Horse Whisperer" and "True Lies". Once the real snow had been spread out from the semi-trucks, the special effects' crew covered it with the white foam giving it the appearance of a pristine snow fall. As night fall came, we had yet to film the early morning scene when our entire family went out to begin shoveling. The producers were prepared for this. We watched with awe as the lighting specialists created a daybreak scene in the midst of pitch darkness. In all, nineteen hours of filming took place on the second day. It ended at 2:00 a.m. with Ruth, Jennifer, Eric, and I sitting on the couch filming our satellite conversation with the show's host, Richard Thomas.

During the second day of filming, *The Pantagraph* sent out a photographer to capture the event on film. Later, Paul Swiech called us for a phone interview. Paul was the same reporter who had interviewed us one year ago for the story published in the paper. Paul started, "I have one question which I need to ask you. Do you remember a year ago, when I asked you how you knew that this was a miracle?"

"I do," I said, "and I already know what you are going to ask. I told you that if this was a miracle, that God would find a way to tell the story and if it wasn't a miracle, then it would die on its own. Yes, I remember, and the answer is no," I continued. "I did not contact the show, *It's a Miracle*. The editors from *Angels on Earth* magazine contacted them." I then told Paul what the producers had shared with us - that they go through 3,000 stories just to choose one. Paul paused on the other line.

"Okay," he said as he continued on with the interview. We believed that Paul's continued coverage of Eric's recovery was another indicator that God wanted us to continue to share the story of His miracle. Over time, Eric was asked to speak with over twenty churches, youth groups, and other organizations to share his story. He boldly spoke to these groups about his experience, the importance of making sure you are right with God, and leading a clean life free of alcohol, tobacco, and drugs.

Later that winter, Eric found himself a starter on the junior varsity basketball squad. It was a far cry from barely playing at all. He shared with us that he still dreamed of playing college basketball and even professionally after that. Since Eric's tumor less than two years ago, he had grown nine inches without gaining a substantial amount of weight. I suggested to him that if playing collegiate basketball was his goal, then he should consider beginning a weightlifting program. Eric told me that he was committed, so I helped help him design a program. The first day Eric was able to bench press a maximum of 135 pounds. I did not really push him. Like everything else, when Eric sets his mind to it, he is relentless until he succeeds. He stayed with the program and gradually his success became evident.

By his junior year Eric was 6'3", weighed 170 pounds, and was bench pressing around 200 pounds. This was a break through year for Eric. As a junior he was now starting on varsity and leading the area in free-throw percentage at 86%.

All of those free throws in the barn were beginning to pay off.

In his best game he scored twenty points against one of his

conference rivals. It would prove to be good enough to receive

an invitation to try out for the U.S.A. Junior Nationals at the

season's end. Out of one hundred boys who tried out sixteen

would make up two Illinois teams. Eric was one of them. With

each success Eric came closer to making his dream a reality.

He wanted a scholarship to play college basketball.

courtesy of James Elliott

Eric takes a shot during his junior year at Olympia High School

# CHAPTER ELEVEN - ACHIEVING THE IMPOSSIBLE

As in most college recruiting processes, much depended on how he prepared during that summer between his junior and senior year. It proved to be his most dedicated summer yet. Eric lifted weights faithfully, followed by hours in the gym playing basketball. He had grown to 6'4" and weighed 185 pounds. His jumping ability had increased to the point that he could now dunk the basketball with ease, and his three point shooting was very consistent.

In July, the Junior Nationals were held in Columbus, Ohio. We were very impressed with the talent pool of many blue chip prospects. Eric's Illinois team started slow but finished very strong, making the sweet sixteen out of fifty-two

total teams. Eric averaged fourteen points per game and nine

rebounds per game, with game highs of twenty-nine points

against Montana and twenty-five points against New Jersey.

Eric dunks the ball at the USA Junior Nationals in Columbus,
Ohio.

Returning to Illinois, Eric had more determination than

ever before. He had played with some of the best players in

the country and was able to not only hold his own, but excel against them. He had done what he could to prepare himself for the important, final high school season.

By the beginning of his senior year, Eric's height seemed to be leveling off, but he continued to gain weight due to his weightlifting program. At the beginning of his final basketball season, several division II schools were watching Eric; however, his senior year would bring a host of new challenges.

The varsity coach was new this year and with the change came a new philosophy. Very rarely did any of the players play more than half of the game. Instead, most of the ten players shared playing time fairly equally throughout the game. Eric led the team in scoring, averaging 9.6 points per game, but it was a far cry from what college scouts were looking for in terms of statistics.

In the middle of the season, Eric received another set back. He was elbowed in the head which created a gash that later required seven stitches and produced a concussion that lasted for the next three weeks. Eric's concussion was so severe that for seven days he could not get up and out of bed without vomiting. Both Ruth and I feared that this might be a career ending injury. Eric, on the other hand, had other ideas. He was bound and determined to make it back before the end of the season. He knew he still had something to prove.

Eric's grit and determination paid off once again. Eric returned for the last home game of the year, senior night, which traditionally meant that all of the seniors would be starting for one last time. Eric came out "hot", wanting to prove that his career was not over. He made five of seven shots including two of two from three point range during the first two quarters of play. The team had built a comfortable eight point lead; however, that was to change. Eric had already played half of the game, which meant that he would not play the rest of the night. The team faltered and eventually lost, but the videotape of the game proved to be more of a benefit to Eric than we realized. Eric had great statistics for only averaging half a game throughout the season and nothing exemplified this more than his last regular season game.

Throughout the year, I had filmed each game on our camcorder, so I compiled Eric's senior season highlights followed by three full games on each tape and then sent them out to various junior college coaches in the Midwest. Within a week we were flooded with phone calls from college coaches. They all commented on the same thing. With Eric's obvious talent, "Why did he not play more than half of each game?" That is why I had sent the videotape. I knew that just telling them about Eric's ability would not have the impact of seeing it firsthand. The videotape was proof of what we told them, which was that we knew all along that Eric had the talent to play college basketball. Prospective coaches could then determine whether or not Eric possessed the talent to play for them. Before the end of the school year Eric had two solid scholarship offers to play for Division II junior colleges.

Before we began our college search, I had not realized there were so many differences in basketball at the junior college level. I found out that Division I schools offered full ride scholarships which included tuition plus room and board. Division II schools could offer full tuition but not room and board, while Division III schools could not offer any athletic assistance, just academic grants and scholarships. Before the end of his senior year, Eric chose Carl Sandburg Junior College in Galesburg, Illinois. For a junior college the school had great facilities, including a new gym and work out center. Eric was especially drawn to the head coach, Mike Bailey, and his assistant coach, Rob Williams. Both had played college basketball at the University of Northern Iowa, a Division I school in the Missouri Valley Conference. Eric and I appreciated their enthusiasm, confidence, and knowledge of the game. Rob is also the nephew of NBA great, Doug Collins. He told us that Doug had been like a second father to him. Doug had passed on to Rob not only his knowledge of basketball but the life lessons he had learned as well.

At the conclusion of Eric's recruiting visit at Carl Sandburg, we sat down to have lunch with the two coaches in the school cafeteria. Eric and I felt that this was a good time to tell them about his past medical history. Eric desperately wanted this chance to play college ball, but he didn't want to accept their offer without making them completely aware of his illness. Though Eric's repeat MRI's had not shown any re-growth in the small piece of tumor which remained, a remote possibility still existed. Coach Bailey immediately responded to our news and said that he had noticed the large scar on the back of Eric's head when he was trying out at one of the open gyms. Coach Bailey assured Eric that his past medical history would have no effect on Eric's scholarship. However, he was quite impressed by it. He said, "I had a brother who had a brain tumor, so I can appreciate the dedication that it must have taken to have that kind of surgery and then bounce back to play competitive basketball again. Quite frankly, that is the kind of dedication that I am looking for from my players," explained Mike.

I knew that most college coaches looked for players who have demonstrated an exceptional work ethic. Coach Bailey's family experience provided him with an immediate understanding of the work involved in Eric's progress as a result of his illness.

However, there were other indicators of how driven Eric was in his desire to improve and excel in college basketball. I told the coaches, "I don't think you will be able to push Eric harder than what he pushes himself." I explained Eric's senior year schedule to them as an example.

Eric awoke at 1:30 a.m. every morning to do a rural paper route. He traveled a total of 90 miles each night and finished at 4:30 a.m. He went back to bed until 7:30 a.m. at which time he had to get up for school. After school, Eric lifted weights in the gym and then played basketball for an hour or two. He came home for dinner, homework, and usually went to bed by 9:00 p.m. During the basketball season, I occasionally helped Eric out with his route. I tried to assist on those evenings he had away games and didn't return home until 11:00 p.m. or later. There were numerous occasions when our schedules conflicted, and I was at work, leaving Eric to fend for himself. It all paid off for him, though, when he was able to purchase a 1999 Chevy S-10 pick-up.

After our discussion with the coaches from Carl Sandburg J.C., they were even more convinced that Eric should be a part of their basketball program. Before we left, Eric made a verbal commitment to attend Carl Sandburg with a full tuition scholarship. Coach Bailey said that he would send the "National Letter of Intent" on the first day allowed by NCAA rules. The drive home from Galesburg went quickly. Eric was on cloud nine! I was happy for him and told him how proud I was of him. "Having your college tuition paid for is quite an honor," I told him. "I'm proud of you for not quitting when the

going got tough," I said with a gentle smile.

photo courtesy of Ray Mendez

Eric playing for Carl Sandburg College after earning a

scholarship.

Having reached his goal to play collegiate basketball,

Eric still didn't quit. He wanted to be successful. The rest

of the school year and into the summer months, Eric hit the

weight room hard. By the end of the summer, he had increased

his bench press immensely, finishing his routine lifting 315 pounds. Not only had he increased his physical strength; he was dunking with ease now, just two steps and he could put the ball down. During the summer, Eric's routine stayed consistent. He still delivered papers every night and then went back to bed by 5:00 a.m. When he woke, he lifted weights for two hours and then played basketball for another two hours.

Eric after years of therapy and weightlifting just one month before starting college.

By June, we had sold our farm and lived in a quiet little cabin, provided to us by some close friends while we built a small house in the town of Normal. Our builder, a good friend from church, was kind enough to let us put a lot of sweat equity into the house. In the month of August, one week before Eric left for college, I asked for his help roofing our new house. He agreed without complaint, but I could tell roofing in 95 degree weather left him exhausted for his workouts. Still, he managed both. I joked with him that if he ever felt like dropping out of college, he should remember how miserable it was putting on those shingles in 95 degree temperatures and 90 percent humidity. "Earning your degree gives you many options and opens many doors, but learning a trade such as roofing is something that will also benefit you the rest of your life," I told him.

By the second week of August, college began. Eric's first semester in school he carried fifteen hours of classes. As college athletes do, he finished classes as early as possible, by

2:00 p.m. every day. Team workouts began shortly after with weightlifting and then open gym for scrimmages. Eric loved his new schedule. It was so much easier than getting up at 1:30 every morning to deliver papers.

A month into this routine, Eric severely sprained his ankle in practice. Although no permanent damage was done, it was bad enough to keep him from playing on it for the next six weeks. Eric was very discouraged and worried that he would not return to his previous jumping form. We had faith in him and knew that he would do everything the rehabilitation therapists advised. Having overcome much bigger obstacles before, recovering from this was relatively easy.

As the weeks passed, the day of the season opener finally arrived. Eric called us the night before the game to let us know that he probably would not start, since the injury had kept him from practicing with the team early on. We told Eric that it didn't matter to us and that we would be at the game regardless of whether he played or not.

As Eric's first college basketball game began, I felt as if I were more nervous than he was. I hoped I was more nervous than he was! It wasn't long before Eric had entered the game and found himself open for a three point shot. As the ball left Eric's hands, it seemed to be traveling toward the basket in slow motion. My heart pounded as I heard the ball swish through the net. Defying all odds Eric had just made his first collegiate basket. Moments later, Eric again found himself open for a three point shot. This time he was four feet beyond the three point line. Filled with confidence from making his first basket, he again shot the ball. Swish!! He had made two in a row!

As Ruth and I stood applauding our son, we were both filled with an overwhelming sense of pride. Any other parents watching their son at that moment would have been proud. Yet I knew that the moment was something much more that even that. I couldn't help but recount in my mind the mountain of obstacles that Eric had overcome to arrive at this day. Most of the spectators who sat in the stands with us would never know that a small piece of the original brain tumor diagnosed in January, 1999 remains. To the fans who watched him or the opponents he faced on the court, he was just one of the many good college basketball players they would see. In fact, that is exactly what Eric wanted them to see.

To me, however, the young man I was watching on that basketball court was the boy who overcame double vision. He was the boy who couldn't run without falling yet now performed aerial acrobatics while driving to the basket. He was the boy who shot the basketball four feet to the right of the rim, who now swished three pointers with consistency. He was the boy who had become a man, who had overcome all obstacles in his path to achieve what all of his doctors said he would never do again.

As I continued to applaud Eric, my eyes welled up with tears. I was overcome with emotion, for I had just witnessed the impossible become reality. By the grace of God and Eric's strong will and determination, I witnessed what many have described as a "miracle".

It seems as if it were just yesterday when we discovered Eric had a brain tumor the size of an orange. In other ways the five years that have since passed, seem to be twenty. We, along with all those people with whom we have shared his story, understand the countless hours of pain, therapy, and training it took for Eric to realize his boyhood dream coming true this night.

The remainder of the season Eric started virtually every game and averaged 10.3 points and 3.5 rebounds per game. His three point shooting average was 38.3%. He contributed 33 assists and 27 steals to his team's totals. Eric's drive and determination have proven that if the dream is big enough, no mountain is too high to climb!

# About The Author

Jeff Elliott is a full-time firefighter for the town of Normal, in Illinois. Married to his wife Ruth for 23 years, they have two children, Jennifer 21, and Eric 19.

CPSIA information can be obtained at www.ICGtesting.com
Printed in the USA
LVOW100230020412

275649LV00024B/1/A